CH

Denham Court, a stately home on the outskirts of London, fell into disrepair in the 1920s, and for many years was used as a youth detention centre. In one room of the dilapidated house hung a dark, dirty painting. Most of the inmates hardly gave it a second look. Some even used it as a dartboard. But then a visitor spotted it…

Looking past the holes and the layers of filth, he saw something that made his heart beat faster, and he carefully lifted it down. Now, restored and repaired, this painting of Peter Rubens' house was displayed in London's National Gallery as a fine example of a 17th-century Dutch master.

The events of the first Christmas often receive similar treatment. Some walk past the familiar figures of angels and shepherds every year without noticing. For them Christmas is about Santa and presents, turkey and fairy lights, time off work, family rows and Christmas specials on TV.

For others that first Christmas scene is useful only as a dartboard. It has no value to them, so they just try to poke holes in it. But is it possible that there is more to this familiar

Christmas story than we think? Perhaps a closer examination will reveal something valuable, even priceless, underneath the crust of neglect?

So let's strip away the dust and grime of the Christmas-card images we have in our minds and get back to the original underneath. What was the *real* Christmas all about? To do that we need to go back to the original eye-witness records in the Bible.

> *This is how the birth of Jesus Christ came about. His mother Mary and Joseph had promised to get married. But before they started to live together, it became clear that she was going to have a baby. She became pregnant by the power of the Holy Spirit. Her husband Joseph was a godly man. He did not want to put her to shame in public. So he planned to divorce her quietly.*
>
> *But as Joseph was thinking about this, an angel of the Lord appeared to him in a dream. The angel said, "Joseph, son of David, don't be afraid to take Mary home as your wife. The baby inside her is from the Holy Spirit. She is going to have a son. You must give him the name Jesus. That is because he will save his people from their sins."*
>
> *All of this took place to bring about what the Lord had said would happen. He had said through the prophet, "The virgin is going to have a baby. She will*

*give birth to a son. And he will be called Immanuel."
The name Immanuel means "God with us."*

*Joseph woke up. He did what the angel of the
Lord commanded him to do. He took Mary home
as his wife. But he did not make love to her until
after she gave birth to a son. And Joseph gave him
the name Jesus.*

from the book of Matthew in the Bible,
chapter 1 verses 18-25

Matthew, the writer of this account of the first Christmas,
understood that it was a unique event. An event which has
implications for all time and all people.

Who's the daddy?

The first unique feature is there at the beginning:

*This is how the birth of Jesus Christ came about.
His mother Mary and Joseph had promised to get
married. But before they started to live together, it
became clear that she was going to have a baby. She
became pregnant by the power of the Holy Spirit.*

Mary gets pregnant before sleeping with her husband Joseph.
In fact, according to Matthew, they didn't actually have sex
until after the birth. Now that is a first!

A little boy was doing a school project on his family tree. He
came home one day and asked:

"Dad, where did I come from?"
The flustered father replied: *"The stork brought you."*
A while later he asked his mother,
"Mum, where did you come from?"
"I was found under a gooseberry bush," she said.
Granny also happened to be staying with them so the little boy asked her, and she too held the line.
"The stork brought me," she said.
Next day, he went back to school and started to write his project. It began: *There hasn't been a normal birth in our family for three generations…*

In the case of Jesus, though, it really *wasn't* a normal birth. Matthew twice records that the child was conceived by the Holy Spirit. Does that seem to you far-fetched? It's not just far-fetched—it's absurd, it's impossible, humanly speaking. But that is precisely the point. The claim is that this was God intervening in a unique way in the world. It was a miracle.

You can't help but feel a bit sorry for Joseph. Put yourself in his shoes. You come home from work one day and your wife says to you: *"I've got two bits of good news and one bit of bad news. The good news is that I'm pregnant. The bad news is that you're not the father. But the good news is that God is."* I think most men in that situation would be a bit sceptical, and Joseph was no exception.

He was clearly no fool, but it seems he *was* a good man. So Matthew records that:

He did not want to put her to shame in public. So he planned to divorce her quietly.

But as Joseph is chewing all this over, we read that an angel of the Lord appears to him in a dream and confirms Mary's version of events. And so he accepts that this *really is* God at work.

Conception and childbirth without sex; an angel appearing in a dream. This is not normal. But no one is claiming that it is. On the contrary. These highly abnormal features mark out the birth of Jesus as something very special—extraordinary in fact. The Christian claim is that Jesus had a unique birth, and that claim alone means this particular painting deserves a closer look.

Advance warning

Now all of us naturally find such extraordinary goings-on difficult to believe, precisely because they are so alien to our own experience. But God knows that. And that's one reason why he gave plenty of advance warning that this was going to take place. Far from being a bolt out of the blue, Matthew tells us:

All of this took place to bring about what the Lord had said would happen. He had said through the prophet, "The virgin is going to have a baby. She will give birth to a son. And he will be called Immanuel." The name Immanuel means "God with us."

That prediction of the virgin birth is to be found in the Old Testament part of the Bible, in the book of Isaiah—written over 700 years before Jesus was born. The prophet Micah, also writing in the 8th century BC, pinpoints that the place of this birth would be Bethlehem, then just a little town of a few hundred people. God revealed the details of this unique birth hundreds of years before it happened, so that when it *did* happen, we would have confidence to believe that these things are true.

Personally, I find the account both persuasive and compelling. Matthew's gospel is clearly written as history not fiction, and by someone who knew Jesus personally. The way it fulfils Old Testament prophecies is very striking. But so what? What is the significance of this unique birth? The significance of the birth lies in the identity of the baby.

A unique baby

From this unique birth came a unique baby. In what way was he unique? We find the answer in the three names he was given.

In the current list of most popular names, various versions of Jacob (shortened to Jack) have been the number one option for the last 15 years. Many parents name their children after the latest celebrity. But it is left to the celebs themselves to get creative with new names. You can't help wondering if Daisy Boo, Chudney and Kal-El Coppola will be thanking their parents in years to come. (They're the children of Jamie Oliver, Diana Ross and Nicolas Cage, if you didn't know).

In Bible times it was the *meaning* of names that was highly significant. A child was given a name that showed its importance, or what parents hoped for the future of the child. The three names given to this baby show us what is at the heart of the real Christmas. They answer three vitally important questions for us:

Immanuel: *Who is the real father?*

First, he is called Immanuel.

> *"She will give birth to a son. And he will be called Immanuel."*

Immanuel is Hebrew for "God with us". The staggering truth contained in that title for the baby born at Christmas is expressed in many of the carols we sing: "He came down to earth from heaven, Who is God and Lord of all" (in *Once in Royal David's City*).

In that first century stable lay a child who was both a real human being and also God. By means of this virgin conception, the human and the divine came together in a unique way. Physically, he was the son of Mary; legally he was the son of Joseph who names him; but at the most fundamental level he was also the Son of God. *God with us.*

If God the Son has come into our world, then it has deep implications. At the very least it tells us that we matter to God. Astronomically, we are as insignificant as specks of dust, bouncing around on an minor planet in a backwater of a gigantic universe. But the birth of 'Immanuel' tells us that we are very much on God's radar screen. We are the visited planet… But it raises the question—*why did God bother?* What was the purpose of the trip?

Jesus: *What is the real problem?*

The answer to that lies in another name he was given, the actual name that he used. The angel says:

> **"She is going to have a son. You must give him the name Jesus. That is because he will save his people from their sins."**

The name Jesus means "God saves". The Son of God came from heaven to save; he came on a rescue mission. And in particular it says he came to rescue us "from our sins".

In a trial one Christmas time the judge asked the defendant, *"What are you charged with?"* The man said: *"Doing my Christmas shopping early."* "But that's no offence," said the judge; *"how early were you doing your shopping?"* The man replied: *"Before the store opened."*

Our sins are the wrong things we do, and the good things we fail to do. Sins are not just breaking the law of the land but breaking the law of God. The law of God which is summed up in the commands to love the Lord your God and to love other people. All of us break these laws.

But these sins are just the symptoms of a bigger disease that infects us all. We are happy to take the wonderful gifts

God gives us: Our life, friendships, our health, talents and abilities. But we want to run our lives our own way. We do not want God ruling over us. Deep down, we are ungrateful rebels against the God who made us and gave us everything we have. And we will be judged for it.

Many of us may make it through life without ever appearing before a judge in Court. But all of us break God's law every day of our lives. And so we need rescuing. Rescuing because these sins cut us off from God—now, and for all eternity.

You may have you heard of the four stages of life.

1. You believe in Santa Claus.
2. You don't believe in Santa Claus.
3. You become Santa Claus.
4. You start to look like Santa Claus…

But what then? The Bible says that *"Man is destined to die once and after that face judgment."* This is a judgment that none of us deserve to escape. But that is why Christmas is such wonderful news for each and every one of us. Christmas is about the birth of the *rescuer* sent from God; sent to die so that we can be forgiven by God and know him for ever.

But the angel says that Jesus will only save *"his people"* from their sins? Isn't that a bit exclusive? Yes and no. Yes, because you have to be one of *"his people"* to benefit. But no, because the invitation to become one of his people is open to everyone. There are no restrictions. All are welcome.

Christ: *What is the real solution?*

The baby is Immanuel, God with us. He is Jesus, the rescuer. And lastly he is the Christ.

Christ is not a surname but a title, like Dr or Professor. The Greek word *Christ*—or the same word in Hebrew *Messiah*—both mean "the anointed one". In the Old Testament "the anointed one" was the king that God had chosen to rule over his people. But the Bible writers looked forward to the day when God would send *the* King, with a capital 'K'. A King not just of a little nation in the middle east, but the King of the whole of God's world.

The very term "*Christ*mas" is an annual reminder that the King has now come; a reminder of who the real boss is—that Jesus is the rightful ruler of our lives. Perhaps that's one reason we prefer a safe and fun X-mas to the real Christmas.

One restaurant near us has a banner at the front saying *"X-mas dinner bookings now taken"*. At one level it makes sense—you can make do with a shorter banner and save money. But there is something in each of us which does want to get rid of the Christ and replace him with an "X". If I want to keep running my own life my own way, the news that the King—the Christ—has come, is not what I want to hear. An "X" leaves me in charge of my own life—at least for the time being. But this is a policy that is heading for disaster. When we finally meet the true King, we will have no defence.

The real Christmas

So this is the real Christmas. It is about who Jesus really is: God's real solution to the real problem with the world. This is the meaning hidden under the layers of dusty familiarity with this story. It is about our real need for forgiveness. It is about God's genuine love for us in sending his only Son to rescue us. It is about who is really in charge of the world today, and how we should respond to him.

So what is your response to this nativity scene? If you're someone who has already worked out that this picture is something of immense value, the challenge may be to have the picture on public display. To be known as one of Jesus' people.

But you may be someone who has just been walking past each year without really noticing the painting. You may even have thrown the occasional dart at it, not really thinking it might be worth anything.

If that's you, why not take a closer look? You could read through one of the gospel accounts; you could check out a local church where the Bible is explained; you could go along to a *Christianity Explored* course which explains some of the fundamentals of the Christian faith; you could talk things over with a Christian friend who gave you this booklet, or start to attend the church where you received it, and think through these important questions.

Or you could accept the invitation to become one of Jesus' people, living for him as your rescuer and your ruler.

Here's a prayer you could pray to take that step:

Lord God, I thank you for the real Christmas.

Thank you that Jesus is Immanuel: God with us. Thank you that he came to rescue me from my sins.

Thank you that he is Christ—who is in charge of the world and calls me to be one of his followers.

I admit that I have failed to live as you command and need rescuing. I am sorry, and put my trust in Jesus as my rescuer.

I admit that I have failed to live with Jesus as my ruler. I am sorry and submit to Jesus as the ruler of my life.

Please become "God with me" now as you come into my life. Amen.